# SPECTACULAR CARDS!

## Fabric, Paper & Game Board Greetings

# Sue Astroth

C&T PUBLISHING

Text © 2005 Sue Astroth

Artwork © 2005 C&T Publishing, Inc.

Publisher: Amy Marson

Editorial Director: Gailen Runge

Acquisitions Editor: Jan Grigsby

Editor: Stacy Chamness

Copyeditor/Proofreader: Wordfirm Inc.

Cover Designer: Kristen Yenche

Design Director/Book Designer: Kristen Yenche

Production Assistant: Matt Allen

Photography: Diane Pedersen and Luke Mulks, unless otherwise noted

Published by C&T Publishing, Inc., P.O. Box 1456, Lafayette, California, 94549

Attention Teachers: C&T Publishing, Inc., encourages you to use this book as a text for teaching. Contact us at 800-284-1114 or www.ctpub.com for more information about the C&T Teachers Program.

We take great care to ensure that the information included in this book is accurate and presented in good faith, but no warranty is provided nor results guaranteed. Having no control over the choices of materials or procedures used, neither the author nor C&T Publishing, Inc., shall have any liability to any person or entity with respect to any loss or damage caused directly or indirectly by the information contained in this book. For your convenience, we post an up-to-date listing of corrections on our web page (www.ctpub.com). If a correction is not already noted, please contact our customer service department at ctinfo@ctpub.com or at P.O. Box 1456, Lafayette, California, 94549.

Trademarked (™) and Registered Trademark (®) names are used throughout this book. Rather than use the symbols with every occurrence of a trademark and registered trademark name, we are using the names only in the editorial fashion and to the benefit of the owner, with no intention of infringement.

Library of Congress Cataloging-in-Publication Data

Astroth, Sue,

Spectacular cards : fabric, paper & game board greetings / Sue Astroth.

p. cm.

Includes bibliographical references.

ISBN 1-57120-310-9 (paper trade)

1. Greeting cards. I. Title.

TT872.A877 2005

745.594'1—dc22

2004029489

Printed in Singapore

10 9 8 7 6 5 4 3 2 1

# Contents

This book is dedicated to Dad. You're always with me.

## Acknowledgments

Once again, my family and friends provided me immense support as I took on this project during difficult times. Without any one of them this project would have ended before it began.

Mom—Thanks for giving me such a wonderful foundation; you taught me everything I know and that's *not* a bad thing!

Phyllis and all my friends at Stamper's Warehouse—Your support, encouragement, samples, constructive suggestions, and most of all your friendships mean the world to me. Thank you all!

Barbara D.—Thank you for your continued support and inspiration. Also, thanks for not needing your Sizzix machine back right away!

Terrece S., Barbara D., Margaret R., Krista H., Debbie D., and Vanessa O.—Thanks for creating and sharing your beautiful artwork!

To Stacy C., Jan G., Liz A., Cyndy R., Mari D., and everyone at C&T—The opportunities, the friendship, the patience, and the encouragement…you guys are the best!

Joseph B.—Yours may be the only artwork shrine dedicated to me outside of my parent's home. Love to you always.

Olaitan C.—You have amazing talents as an artist and as a dear friend. Thank you for always being willing to share.

Elena M.—You are far and above the most enthusiastic agent I have in San Jose! Thank you for your friendship, you are truly wonderful. (Gregory, you're not too bad either!)

Corey C., Erin C., Megan P., Melanie P, and all the kids who provided photos for the Teacher's game board—Way cool! You guys made an ordinary card really special.

Jois—It is your friendship, love, encouragement, and support that have given me the confidence to walk through the doors that have opened for me. Being able to do what I really enjoy is the best. Thank you, still!

We are the sum total of our life's experiences—so is our art. Thank you to all the artists who continue to make art for everyone to enjoy and grow ideas of our own. I appreciate your talent and ability to continue creating something "new."

## Why Cards?

Greeting cards allow people to send special messages of love and friendship to each other. These messages come in many forms. Most are made of a paper card decorated with color and embellishments, all geared to make the recipient smile. Some cards, however, come in different forms…a message in a box, a fabric-covered greeting, even an altered game board. The purpose of this book is to provide you with a map and some inspiration so you can begin to create your own greetings that will bring smiles and giggles to your family and friends.

In this world of electronic communication and cell phones, greeting cards, especially handmade ones, have a special place in my heart. Although it is wonderful to be able to get in touch with someone almost immediately, there is nothing quite like the excitement of finding a letter or card in the mailbox. I still get a thrill when I hear the sound of the mail truck. I never know what treasures may await me. I love the anticipation; I even get excited at the arrival of mail at work!

I have been making cards for family members for years. Over the years the cards have become a bit more sophisticated. Early examples included cut-up construction paper and crayons. Though as a youngster I always tried to color *inside* the lines, with age and maturity I have found that coloring *outside* the lines can definitely lead to bigger and better things!

Homemade cards and letters are a wonderful way to cheer up someone you can't be near. I enjoy all aspects of creating a card for someone special; the planning, treasure collecting, and the creative process where the idea becomes real (though sometimes different than the original design you had in mind). Sometimes I make the task of creating a card monumental. I'll add one more embellishment here, a ribbon there, maybe another layer of paper…but I know I'm just adding more fun, friendship, and love.

I've come a long way from the crayons and construction paper of my early years. In this book I show you how to take small cuts of fabric, paper scraps, and various embellishments both old and new to create beautiful cards and greetings to send your family and friends. I hope you will find some new ideas and twists on old tried-and-true methods of making greeting cards.

I've tried to include sources for the wonderful embellishments, stamps, and so on that I use in these cards, but sometimes that isn't possible. I collect card-making "treasures" constantly. Whenever I see something useful, unique, or interesting I'll grab it to use in a card at some point. Some of my treasures have come from garage sales, flea markets, and second-hand stores, or are items I've found while on a walk. In these instances a vendor name isn't available, but it shouldn't be hard for you to find something comparable!

# The basics

There are so many great art, scrapbook, and quilting products on the market today! Now more than ever we have tons of choices, and the division line between the projects are fading. Thanks to scrapbooking, there is a lot of crossover between the various mediums.

I'm a fabric collector (oops, I mean *quilter*) from way back. Exactly how far back doesn't really matter. Suffice it to say I am fortunate to have lots of fabric and quite a few finished quilts. In an effort to use up some more of the woven treasure I had accumulated, I wrote *Fast, Fun & Easy Scrapbook Quilts*. It was a wonderful journey and experience. Not only did I get to play with fabric and make new friends, I was also able to include some of my new passions: rubber stamps, vintage embellishments, and paper! All these mediums went so well together for the quilts that I figured they could work for greeting cards, too.

## STAMPS, INKS, EMBOSSING, AND PAPER
### Stamps

In the world of rubber stamps you can find anything from a cute teddy bear to the Mona Lisa, and just about everything in between. These images—combined with stamped sayings using equally diverse alphabets—make for great cards. Check out Sources (see page 76) for some of my favorite stamp companies.

So many wonderful alphabet stamp sets are available that it's hard to believe you would need your computer to help you make cards, but you do! The computer helps format greeting cards or invitations with the ease of pushing a couple buttons. It also makes many various fonts available to you, usually in several sizes. You can purchase font software for your computer from many shops, such as art or scrapbook stores. These jam-packed software discs are usually easy to use and provide you with lots of choices. Also something to consider is the availability of free fonts online. Type "free fonts" into a search engine online and you'll be sure to find lots of styles from various sites. If you are like me, you will see quite a few you like. Be aware—fonts take up lots of memory—so be sure you have enough space on your computer, or consider downloading them onto a disc. Also, to help prevent infecting your computer, make sure to scan the files for viruses when you download anything from the Internet.

**Dye-based ink**: These water-based inks dry quickly on absorbent paper. They offer a good color selection, and they are sheer so they can be used to add color to a stamped image. They wash easily with soap and water.

**Pigment-based ink**: These inks are slow-drying; can be heat set; offer a good, opaque color selection; are good for creating interesting backgrounds; and are excellent for embossing images. They also wash easily with soap and water.

**Permanent inks**: These solvent-based inks offer a limited color selection, but they are excellent for stamping on non-porous surfaces. These inks require solvent ink cleaner.

As with all things, the art supply manufacturers keep coming up with new formulations of ink to keep us coming back for more! A couple of the latest versions are *chalk inks* and *hybrid inks*. The chalk inks are pigment-based inks that dry more quickly than regular pigment and leave a chalky look to the finished product. They are great for creating backgrounds. Hybrid inks combine the properties of pigment ink with a mica powder. The mica adds an extra sheen and highlight to the ink and your stamped images.

## TIP

Although several good stamp cleaners are on the market, the easiest way to clean ink from your stamps is to have a wet paper towel in a small dish next to you. When you are finished stamping a project, wipe the stamp clean on the paper towel and set it aside to dry.

## Embossing

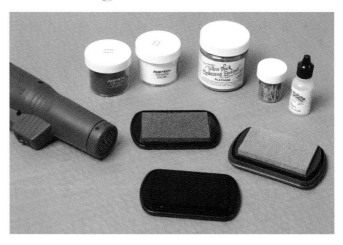

To emboss your image you need to use a special embossing powder (which is actually a fine-ground plastic) in conjunction with either a pigment ink (in color) or an embossing ink (available in clear or tinted) and a heat tool. The color ink you choose will affect your finished result. Using colored ink will add some intensity to the finished product. It's a good idea to test your powder, ink, and cardstock combination before using it on your finished piece.

The embossing process is a simple one:

1. Stamp your images onto your paper with ink.

2. Shake embossing powder over the image before the ink dries, making sure to cover the entire stamped area.

3. Tap off any excess powder.

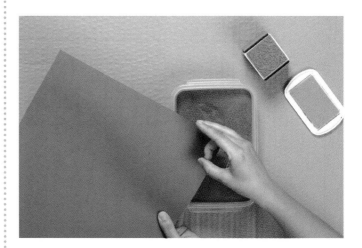

A good whack on the back of the paper is the most effective way to tap off the excess powder.

**4.** Use a heat tool and heat the image until the embossing powder melts, creating a surface sheen. Be careful not to keep the image under the heat tool too long or you may burn the paper.

There are three types of embossing powder:

**Detail**: This very fine powder results in a fine outline of your image. It is great to use for highlighting an image that will be colored with paints, pencils, or chalks.

**Regular**: This medium-grind plastic powder results in an outline when heated.

**Ultra-thick**: This coarse powder creates a very bumpy or moonlike surface when heated with a heat gun. Repeat layers must be added for more complete coverage.

## Paper

One of the reasons I started going into stamping and scrapbook stores was the paper. It's like candy or fabric—gorgeous, gotta-have-it stuff. Cardstock, heavier than copy or computer paper, is good for card making, and typically comes in 8½″ × 11″ and 12″ × 12″ sheets. Sometimes you may find a shop selling small 4¼″ × 5½″ half sheets. Decorative papers and some solid colors are available in larger sheets, around 20″ × 30″. These are usually found in art supply or specialty paper stores.

### NOTE

Most paper has a grain similar to fabric. This is important to know because the grain affects how you make folds, tears, and cuts in your paper. Folding cardstock *with* the grain makes a clean neat fold; folding *against* the grain, as it implies, still gives you a fold but the paper fights back a bit. To check your cardstock for the direction of the grain, try slightly bending the piece of cardstock in both hands. You will definitely notice that one direction—with the grain—bends much more easily and is more noticeable in a heavier-weight cardstock. Tearing a piece of the paper is another way to determine grain; this works better for thinner paper. Tearing against the grain gives you a much more ragged tear as opposed to tearing with the grain. Remember to follow the path of least resistance when making your cuts, tears, and folds.

It is hard to know how much paper a project will require. I typically buy cardstock in large quantities. I like certain colors and use them repeatedly, so I don't want to run out in the middle of a project. I get around ten sheets of 8½″ × 11″ (at least six of a solid color) and two or three sheets of 12″ x 12″ decorative, printed cardstock, or more if I really like the design or have a specific project in mind. With two sheets of decorative paper, you can use one for the card and the second to make a matching envelope. It's also fun to mix and match patterns, like making a small quilt! Because I'm not always sure how I will use the paper, the above numbers give me enough so I don't run out in the middle of a project—whatever it may be!

### NOTE

When purchasing solid-color cardstock, you have two choices. One style has a white center because the color is applied to both sides of a white sheet of base stock. The other style of cardstock is the same color throughout because the pulp is actually dyed before it is made into individual sheets of paper. Each will give your finished project a slightly different look. Play with both to see what you like best.

Also in the paper department are various dimensional "papers" for use in your art projects. Grass cloth, thin metals, wallpaper, open weave mesh, and stiffened fabric have all hit the market and are a great way to add some interest to your cards, books, and game boards.

## TIP

Sometimes when you need paper to match your project, the best way to get that is to take a plain sheet of paper and decorate it yourself.

1. Paint it with metallic or acrylic paint;
2. Swipe your ink pads directly across the paper; or
3. Stamp images all over your sheet of cardstock to create your own stamped background.

You can also take printed scrapbook paper and add some new interest by brushing on a sheer paint or wash, spraying them with walnut ink, or adding some gold leaf. Take the ordinary to the extraordinary!

## TIP

If you ever feel you have too much paper (it could happen!) or you no longer like some of the paper you have, you can always sell the paper at a local stamp or scrapbook swap meet, trade it with a friend, or donate it to a local school or youth organization. This way you'll always have room for more.

# Things to Do with Paper
## *Crimp It!*

Putting wire or thin sheets of metal through your crimper makes for interesting embellishments.

## *Crumple It!*

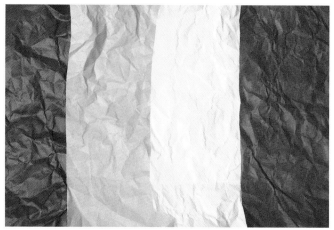

Crumple the paper, then smooth it out with your hands. You could also wipe an inkpad lightly over the crinkles to add color or give your project a vintage look.

## Sand It!

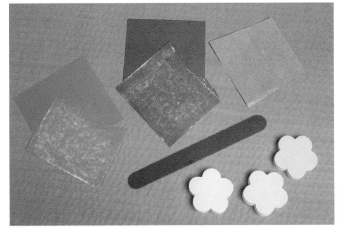

Sanding can be done all over or just on the edges for that "less than new" look that has become so popular. Sand paper much like you would a piece of wood, following the grain. This technique is especially effective with textured and white-centered paper.

## Tear It!

When tearing without the aid of a ruler, the look of the finished edge will depend on which direction you tear the unwanted part of your cardstock away. Tearing the unwanted piece of cardstock toward you will give you a deeper rough tear showing more of the inside of the paper—my personal favorite. Deckle-edged rulers, though sometimes a bit pricey, can be lots of fun to use, and provide a more uniform tear.

## Layer It!

Another type of paper to consider in your card making is *vellum*. This is a fine parchment-style paper that allows you to see through to what is behind the vellum. It is great for layering over printed-paper to mute the print or for stamping on to layer over a print or photo. It also makes a great first page in a card or book. Another fun thing to do with vellum is to make an envelope for your card creations. This gives the recipient a sneak peek at what's inside.

### TIP

One of the challenges of working with vellum is how to attach it to another sheet of paper. My favorite way is to use eyelets or ribbon. Tape will work but you will see the tape, or at least a shadow, through the vellum. One way to eliminate this shadow is to make your piece of vellum a sticker by using a special machine called a Xyron. These machines are available at your local stamp and craft shops.

Paper isn't just for layering anymore, though that is one of my favorite things to do with it! Layering is so simple and can take a card from nice to wow! There are so many techniques to really make your paper work for you.

A lot has been said about acid-free versus non-acid free papers. I usually purchase acid-free papers, though occasionally I will want to include a paper treasure in my art (such as a page from an old book or an old photo) that falls into the acidic category. For cards—possible throwaway items—I'm not too concerned. For game boards and book-related items I do take a bit more care. I use embellishments regardless of their acidity; there are several different things I can do to be able to include the items. I can spray the item with a preservative spray or place the offender in a buffer such as an envelope or pocket made from acid-free stock. Other options are to make a photo transfer or photocopy of the item. Most scrapbook companies make their supplies, both paper and 3-D embellishments, acid-free in order to prevent the deterioration of the artist's work over time. This allows memories to live on for future generations. The companies usually clearly mark their products "acid-free." If this is an important feature for you, and the product isn't marked, contact the company to clarify. Better safe than sorry!

## Cutting Tools

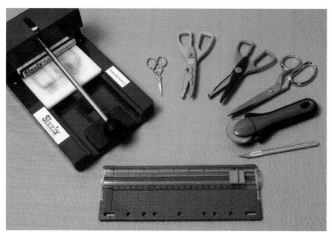

You can't talk about paper without talking about the tools used to cut it!

### Scissors

You can never have too many scissors! I have several pairs for paper, smaller ones for cutting out stamped images and paper dolls, ones with nonstick blades for tape, some for fabric, some for trimming threads at the sewing machine, one pair dedicated only to cutting unmounted stamps, and a bunch of decorative design scissors for paper. The most important thing to remember is to keep your fabric and paper scissors clearly marked and never use your fabric scissors on paper, or vice versa. Paper dulls the blade too much to use the scissors effectively on fabric.

### Rotary Cutters

My studio is always set up for me to cut fabric with a rotary cutter, a clear ruler, and a self-healing cutting mat. One day when clearing these things away to cut paper, I realized I could use the same "fabric" tools for paper. I just made sure I had two rotary cutters, one for fabric and one for paper.

### Paper Cutters

Another great tool on the market today is the personal paper cutter. These little tools are easily transported and allow you to cut photos and paper with built-in rulers to ensure the correct size and cut.

### Sizzix

You know all those great die cuts you can make at your local stamp and craft shops? Well, the Sizzix is a personal die cut machine that lets you make all those great die cuts at home! They are so easy to use and now have the capability to dry emboss as well—simply wonderful! The company has made many different dies (shapes) for you to choose from. My favorites are the basic shapes that I use over and over again—squares, tags, and circles.

### Craft Knives

A craft blade is another must in the studio. Use it to trim away those little bits of paper too small to remove with a personal paper trimmer. A good rule of thumb is to use a metal-edged, clear ruler to guide you when making your cut with the craft knife. That way the knife won't nick your ruler or, more importantly, *you*!

# Other Tools That Come in Handy

**Bone folder**: Coming in a variety of sizes, this tool is a must for all paper and book projects. Use it to help make clean folds in your cards by first scoring along the fold using a ruler as a guide, then scraping the edge of the bone folder along the paper fold to flatten it. The bone folder is also good for smoothing paper that is being glued to another flat surface.

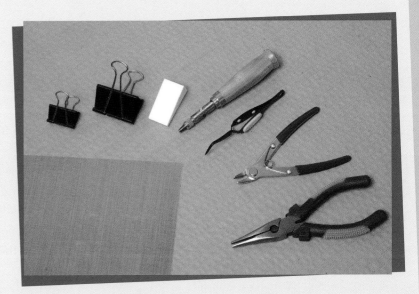

**Clamps**: Sometimes when creating 3-D art, it is hard to glue an item exactly where you want it without getting globs of glue everywhere. The clamp, your typical office supply variety available in several sizes, will help hold the embellishment in place, freeing up your hands so you can move on to the next step.

**Make-up sponges**: These are great tools for creating backgrounds, painting, even adding pastel highlights. Use them to add little wisps of paint to paper for a chalky or antique look.

**Nonstick craft sheet**: I have one or two set up on my stamping desk all the time. If you accidentally get paint or ink directly on it, the sheet allows for easy cleanup—my kind of tool!

**Pliers**: These come in handy when you want to attach charms to your artwork.

**Reverse-action tweezers**: These are good for picking up small eyelets or stamped images, or for holding paper while embossing.

**Shank removers**: These remove the shanks from buttons so the button lays flat and is easier to glue to your artwork.

**Screw punch**: The punch is expensive, but this tool is worth its weight in gold. This little gem allows you to place a hole wherever you want it on your project. It is excellent for eyeletting and various handmade book projects. Be sure to put down a hard protective mat because screw punches are powerful and will put a hole in your cutting mat or desk surface. When I refer to "drilling a hole," this is the tool I use to do just that.

**Wire cutters**: Most craft wire can be cut with your craft scissors but using wire cutters prevents nicking a good pair of scissors.

# ADHESIVES

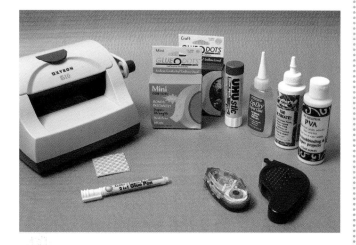

So many glues and adhesives are on the market today that they can take up a whole aisle at your local craft store. Here is a list of what I like to have on hand.

**The Ultimate!** This is a thick, white, tacky glue that dries clear. It is easy to apply with your finger, a brush, or (my favorite) a toothpick. You only need a *very* small amount to adhere paper and cardstock to your fabric cards and game boards. This is an excellent glue to attach heavy 3-D embellishments such as metal letters, watchcases, and keys.

**PVA** This glue is typically used by book artists to adhere decorative papers to their book covers because it seems to minimize any warping the decorative paper may want to do. It is easy to apply with a brush; an expired gift or credit card; or a stiff piece of cardboard for an overall, thin, even coverage.

**Diamond Glaze** This is a dimensional glue that is typically used for adding highlights to your stamped images. It goes on and dries clear. It is excellent for gluing glass embellishments, such as optical lenses or beads, to your art. You can add dye-based inks to this product for added interest.

**Tape Runners** These glue applicators are the best invention for paper crafters on the market. So easy to use, just run the little tool along the edge of your paper and the glue is set in place! These tools come with several options: continuous glue, little tabs, permanent, and removable. The applicators and refills may be a bit pricey, but for me the convenience outweighs the cost.

**Zip Dry** This fast-drying glue is great for gluing paper to paper. I prefer it when gluing paper to the inside of game boards because it is fast and economical. Just remember to use it sparingly and to move quickly!

**Glue Dots** Like little sticky gems, these are super for adhering paper and metal objects onto paper crafts. They peel off a strip and may be a bit tricky to use the first time—read the instructions and don't use your fingers; it lessens the strength of the adhesive bond. The only downside I have found is they seem to slip on art that is displayed standing up.

**Glue Sticks** I use these handy little sticks when I am going to sew paper together. A little dab in the middle of the two papers is just enough to hold the papers together so they won't move. By placing the glue in the middle, it won't be in the path of my stitches or create a mess in my sewing machine. These are also great for gluing lots of pages together in an altered book.

**Glue Pens** This product is a great way to add words, signatures, or thin accents of glitter or embossing to your artwork.

**Xyron Machine** This little hand-operated tool allows you to run ribbon, paper, vellum, or pictures through it and puts adhesive on their back, turning them into decals. It is easy to operate, and with a variety of cartridges to choose from (adhesive, lamination, or magnet) it makes many of your projects very easy to complete.

# FIBERS AND RIBBONS

**Fibers** Who knew what we used to call yarn would get so popular, and for something other than knitting! The fiber colors and textures are perfect additions to add a special finishing touch to your greeting. Fibers are available in yarn shops, your local scrapbook store, thrift shops, and art supply and craft shops.

**Ribbons** A fun way to add color and dimension to greetings. Use them to tie tags on, wrap around paper embellishments, and add little bits of color to the edge of a card. I have a fondness (some say *obsession*) for vintage seam binding. The old treasure can be used just like ribbon. The colors are vibrant and offer a feel of "vintage" times. I mix and match ribbons, seam binding, and fibers all together for a fun, eclectic look. The mix makes a great finish for the fabric books you'll see later in this book. Just about anything you can do with fibers, you can do with ribbon.

**Twill Tape** This is making a comeback—paper artists now use twill tape as a ribbon embellishment. What was once only available in black, natural, and white now comes in all colors of the rainbow, stamped with words or sayings, and in several sizes to suit your card-making, scrapbooking, paper-crafting, or fabric-art needs.

**Twine and Sisal** More fibers to consider including in your card-making stash. You can find these "natural" ribbons at office supply and hardware stores. Even some scrapbook stores now make them available.

# EMBELLISHMENTS

I define an embellishment as anything you add to decorate your base card. So besides the materials for the base card, that leaves almost everything else! Scrapbook stores abound with treasures made especially to add to your artwork. Metal charms, funky alphabets, 3-D paper treasures, wire designs, and even zippers are all available for you to finish off your project.

Keep your artistic eyes and mind open to see what might be available to add to quilts or cards. Treasure-hunting excursions can include junk shops, thrift stores, online auctions, dollar stores (stores that sell goodies for $1 or less), garage sales, swap meets, and church or other organization rummage sales. You never know where you will find the perfect addition to include in your artwork.

Don't consider only what the intended purpose of an item *is*—think of what it *could be*.

Other things I like to use are old game pieces and playing cards, old buttons, keys, snaps, fabric trims, pearl buttons, jewelry scraps, and pages from old books. Another great place to track down some crafting treasure is the hardware store. Here you can look for interesting washers, spray or textured paint, wire, screening, keys, chain, and twine.

One of the easiest places to find treasures is just outside your door. All you have to do is take a walk; twigs, flowers, a lost earring, a penny, and even rocks are fun and surprising elements to add to your art. One of my favorite embellishments is a small, heart-shaped rock I used on one of my scrapbook quilts.

Now that we have reviewed some of the basic tools and embellishments, where to find them, and suggested ways to use them, let's jump into the projects!

# Fabric Cards

A New House...

HAPPY BIRTHDAY TO YOU

I got the idea to try making a fabric card while I was finishing an appliqué sweatshirt for my niece. I made lots of appliqué sweatshirts for family gifts and boutiques so I always had a few extra pieces of the fabric left over. I have a need to recycle everything, so I tried to figure how I might be able to use the leftovers. The shirt was a gift, so a card was definitely the next order of business. I tried one card by folding cardstock and ironing the appliqué to the front of the card. It was a fine, useable card, but I knew I could do better. After some trial and error, I came up with a double-sided fabric card. Wow! It held its shape because I added a good-quality copy paper as a base. I could cut it into any shape, I could sew it, or glue it. I was ready to start makin' cards!

Fabric cards are easy to create and are a great way to use up some of your leftover scraps. I tend to think a "new" project requires some "new" fabric, so if you are like me and want to start at the fabric store, look out! The fabric companies are ready for us, and they have interesting patterns and companion prints to make wonderful cards for just about every occasion. A couple of fat quarters are all the fabric you need to make a couple of basic cards. When buying off the bolt I usually purchase a third of a yard, enough for three cards. I buy more if the pattern is a plaid, stripe, or other one-way design that will require more material to match the fabric design.

## TIP

Sometimes I get overly excited and start making a card—letting the patterns in the fabric guide me. By doing this I sometimes end up with a card outside of the standard envelope size range. No problem! You either buy a larger envelope or make one to fit your latest creation. See Finishing Up (page 73).

# WHAT SIZE?

Once you select the fabric for the card, you'll need some dimensions. I use premade cards as my templates because using standard sizes means envelopes will be readily available.

|  | Cut | Finished/Folded |
|---|---|---|
| Small | 5½" x 8" | 5½" x 4" |
| Large | 6¾" x 9¾" | 6¾" x 4⅞" |
| Money pocket | 9¾" x 7½" | 9¾" x 3¾" |
| String tie | 14½" x 3⅞" | 6" x 3⅞" |
| Giftcard | 3½" x 13" | 3½" x 5" |
| Gift books | 6" x 12" <br> 5" x 14" | 6" x 6" <br> 5" x 7" |
| Double-sided book | 8½" x 15" | 8½" x 5" |
| Accordion | 6" x 40" | 6" x 5" |

# STARTING OUT

Several different fabric adhesive products are on the market, but my favorite is HeatnBond UltraHold Iron-on Adhesive. You can find this product at your local fabric store. It comes in a 17" width but can be overlapped about ¼" to allow you to work on larger areas of fabric or use up some fabric adhesive scraps.

## Supplies

2 pieces of fabric at least 7" × 10"

2 pieces of fabric adhesive the same size as your fabric

1 large sheet of paper to use as lining

Iron and ironing board

Rotary cutter

Clear acrylic ruler

Sewing machine

## TIP

I use a good-quality, 70-pound paper as lining, available at paper stores in a variety of sizes and colors.

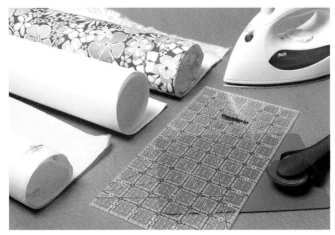

Gather your supplies.

## Preparing the Fabric

1. With a dry iron, iron the fabric adhesive to your fabric.

2. Let it cool, remove the paper backing, and iron the fabric to both sides of the lining paper.

## TIP

For this card sample, I selected a smaller piece of fabric to show the making of just one card. Usually, I let my base-paper size dictate the size of my fabric and fabric adhesive. By doing this, I limit the number of little leftover pieces hanging around in my studio and I will be able to make several cards at one time.

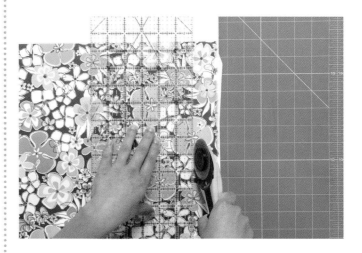

3. Once the adhesive cools, cut the prepared fabric-and-paper piece into the size you need.

## TIP

To make it easier to fold, warm the adhesive before you fold it by ironing both sides of the card.

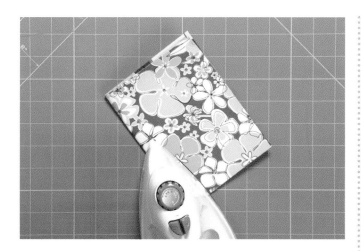

4. Fold the card in half using your iron or a bone folder.

5. Once your card is folded, finish the edges using a decorative stitch. Begin stitching at the fold in the card so when you backstitch it won't be as noticeable.

TIP

For some fun and extra decoration, stitch around the card edge again with a different stitch. Consider using a different color or even a metallic thread to add some pizzazz to your greeting.

TIP

My current favorite is the overlock stitch, but a zigzag stitch will work almost as well. Play with your sewing machine and see which stitches work best for you. Make a sampler of your various edge stitches so you can easily see your choices when you get ready to stitch your card.

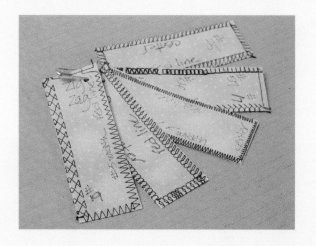

TIP

I prefer an all-cotton thread to match or complement my overall design. Typically I use the same thread color in both the needle and bobbin threads, but I may use different thread colors if the inside and outside fabrics vary dramatically. I use a #12 or #14 needle and I leave the stitch length alone. For artistic balance you may want to decrease the width of the stitch. You can do this with the width button on the machine, or simply move the card over on the throat plate.

All the projects use the prepared fabric we showed you above, cut into various card base sizes. However, the sizes of all of these cards can change to suit your needs. Remember you may have to add or delete some embellishments to keep your card artistically balanced.

# BIRTHDAY

It is hard to select just a few fabrics for birthday cards—there are so many good ones! From bright numbers for the kid at heart to '50s martinis to soft, sweet terra-cotta roses, I think I'm set for cards for the year!

## Batik Roses

This card opens in the middle to be a little different.

**Finished size:** 6" × 6"

### Supplies

Prepared fabric (see page 18)

Peach and rust cardstocks: Bazzill

String tie: EK Success

Happy Birthday stamp: Jody Poesy

Rust color ink: Marvey

## '50s Martini

This one is for my buddy who collects vintage bar ware. To complete the gift, I included a *Cheers!* bookmark.

**Finished size:** 3¾" × 8¾"

### Supplies

Prepared fabric (see page 18)

Light and dark green, off-white, and a scrap of light blue cardstocks: Bazzill

Martini & shaker stamp: The Cat's Pajamas

Happy Birthday stamp: Catslife Press

Metal wine charm: Paper Bliss

Circle punch: EK Success

Light green ink: Marvey

## It's Your Day!

Here is a fun card using chess-inspired fabric. This fabric isn't just for birthdays, it's great for all sorts of cards. Just think of the different captions you could use: "It's Your Move," "The Game of Life," or "Let's Play," to name a few.

**Finished size:** 4¾" × 6⅞"

### Supplies

Prepared fabric (see page 18)

Black-and-white cardstock: Bazzill

Gray thread (Black thread would be too bold.)

Domino button: JHB

Queen stamp: Stamper's Anonymous

Alphabet stamps: Hero Arts

Black wire trim

## 29 Again?

I love the numbered novelty fabric on this card!

**Finished size:** $8\frac{3}{4}'' \times 3\frac{3}{4}''$

## *Supplies*

Prepared fabric (see page 18)

Yellow, purple, and lime green cardstocks: Colormates

Letters and numbers: Sizzix die cuts

8 brads (4 lime green and 4 purple): Making Memories

## #th Birthday

Using another numbered novelty fabric, this is a great card for people who don't want to admit their actual age.

**Finished size:** $3\frac{3}{4}'' \times 8\frac{3}{4}''$

## *Supplies*

Prepared fabric (see page 18)

Cream, blue, and green cardstocks: Colormates

Present charm: Paper Bliss

4 olive green brads: Lasting Impressions

Cut a piece of the prepared fabric $3\frac{1}{2}'' \times 8''$, cutting one of the short sides at an angle. Then sew the piece to the inside of your card. This makes a great pocket for a message tag, a letter, or a gift certificate.

# MORE IDEAS
## Get Well

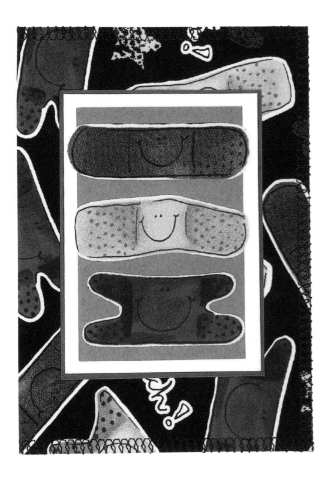

For this card I decided to use the images in the fabric as my embellishments. I applied fabric adhesive to the back side of a scrap of the fabric, cut out the bandages, removed the paper backing, and applied the images to layered cardstock on the front of the card. This technique is a great way to use up some of your "Why did I buy that?" fabric.

**Finished card:** $4\frac{3}{4}" \times 6\frac{3}{4}"$

## Supplies

Prepared fabric (see page 18)

Red, white, and blue cardstocks

## Dog House

My friend Terrece is a talented artist, and after showing her some of my fabric cards, she was off and running. Being a dog lover, she used a dog-theme material as the embellishment to a fun, easy-to-cut dog house card. The roof was cut freehand to fit along the front top of the card.

**Finished size:** $5\frac{1}{2}" \times 5"$ along the sides; 6" at the peak.

## Supplies

Prepared fabric (see page 18)

Wood sticker scrap for "angel" name base

Rub-on letters: Making Memories

## Cowgirl Up!

Terrece couldn't stop at one card. Besides being a dog lover, she is a cowgirl at heart. Her collection of cowboy boots inspired her to make a card in the shape of a boot. Each boot is a pocket with paper "socks" inside. Terrece drew the basic shape for the boot freehand.

## Sew What's New?

A book about cards from a quilter wouldn't be complete without a couple of versions to send to your sewing friends!

**Finished size:** 5″ × 7″

### Supplies

Prepared fabric (see page 18)

White, black, yellow, red, green cardstocks: Bazzill

Snaps or other sewing related treasures

Alphabet stamps: Hero Arts and Making Memories

Acrylic paint

Sewing-related stamps

## For You

With "sew" many sewing-related stamps out there, I couldn't stop at just one card!

**Finished size:** *5" × 7"*

## Supplies

Prepared fabric (see page 18)

White and black cardstocks: Bazzill

Dress form stamp: Stamp in the Hand

Tape measure stamp: B Line Designs

Alphabet stamps: Hero Arts

Button stamp: Catslife Press

Black embroidery thread: DMC

Tag: Sizzix die cut

Sewing machine stamp

## New Home

This fabric was perfect to make a new-house card! A bit of "fussy cutting"—specifically cutting out one image or section of fabric—will get the house in just the right spot.

**Finished size:** *4" × 5½"*

## Supplies

Prepared fabric (see page 18)

Green and cream cardstocks: Colormates

Gold-leafing pen: Sakura Pen-touch

Alphabet stamps: Hero Arts

¼"-wide green satin ribbon

Key

# Thank You

A buddy of mine is a real wine aficionado. When I saw this wine-related fabric I knew it would make the prefect thank-you card for all the great wines he shares with me. This card is a tri-fold card.

**Finished size:** 4″ × 7″

## Supplies

Prepared fabric (see page 18)

Metal letter tiles: Making Memories

Metal photo corners: Art Accents by Provo Craft

Wine-related stamps: Rubber Baby Buggy Bumpers, Great Impressions

Wine charm (from a set of wine charms, bought at a dollar store)

Cream parchment and black cardstocks

Colored pencils (to color the wine in the glass)

You could also use the basic shape of this tri-fold card to make a wallet-style card. Once you have folded the card in thirds, sew the bottom third to the back of the card along each side, creating a pocket.

## TIP

Sometimes the first impression of an inked stamp is too dark for your intended purpose. Here is how to get the right image every time: Ink your stamp and stamp it several times without re-inking on a scrap of the paper you will be using in your project. From this sample piece you can decide which impression will work best in your art.

fig. 1    fig. 2    fig. 3    fig. 4

# NOVELTY-FABRIC CARDS

Novelty-fabric cards are great for kids because they are bright, fun, and whimsical. With so many great prints to choose from, you won't be able to make just one!

## Pink Circles

With its fun, bright colors and circle theme, this card is bound to make a friend smile! A pocket on the last page can hold birthday wishes, some cash or a giftcard, guaranteed to make their smile brighter.

**Finished size:** 3½" diameter

### Supplies

Prepared fabric (see page 18) circles: Sizzix die cuts

Four coordinating 3½" diameter paper circles: Sizzix die cuts

Assorted smaller concentric circles for embellishments: Sizzix die cuts

Happy birthday stamp: Catslife Press

½ yard of ¾"-wide sheer ribbon

Alphabet stamps: Hero Arts

### NOTE

This card is made up of a number of pages. We've taken the card apart to show all the pages.

# Dog Birthday

For a pet lover in your life…
or maybe even for a pet!

**Finished size:** 3¾" × 8½"

## Supplies

Prepared fabric (see page 18)

Blue, white, pink, and yellow cardstocks: Bazzill

Dog and bone buttons: JHB

Scrap of embroidery thread or thin ribbon

## Alternate Version

As a personal challenge, I wanted to make one of the fabric cards different using only what I could reach on my desk. (This challenge is infinitely easier if you tend to be a bit of a cluttered artist!) For a little variation on the 3¾" × 8¾" card, I made a couple slits in the prepared fabric card base. I made the slit about 2" and 3" down from the top of the card, 2"–2½" centered across, and about ¾" apart. I slid a piece of stamped cardstock through these slits and embellished with various treasures and fibers. Try this, and you'll be surprised what you can come up with!

# Teacher Card 101

The combination of fabrics and great buttons makes these cards fast and easy for a quick teacher thank-you. Tuck a giftcard or bookmark inside, and you have a complete gift package!

**Finished size:** $4\frac{7}{8}'' \times 6\frac{3}{4}''$

## Supplies

Prepared fabric (see page 18)

White, red, yellow, green, and blue cardstocks: Bazzill

Apple button: La Mode—Blumenthal Lansing Company

# For You, Teacher

For the many teachers we have in our lives, one card is never enough.

**Finished size:** $3\frac{3}{4}'' \times 8\frac{1}{2}''$

## Supplies

Prepared fabric (see page 18)

Black, yellow, and red cardstocks

Alphabet: Stampotique Originals

Chalkboard button: JHB

$\frac{3}{8}''$-wide red sheer ribbon

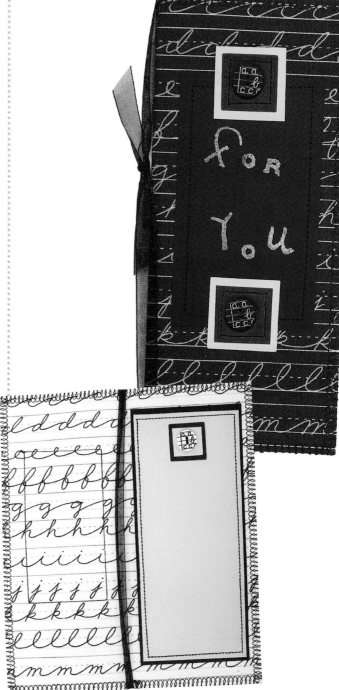

## Old Photos

I love to use old photos in my artwork. The rich brown and sepia tones, the beautiful or interesting clothes, and the priceless expressions all make for great art.

**Finished size:** $3\frac{7}{8}'' \times 6''$

### Supplies

Prepared fabric (see page 18)

Old gold, shiny black cardstocks

Queen stamp: Rubberstamp Ave.

Crown charm

Vintage black button

Black cording for the front tie (Crochet cord works great for this!)

The string-tie look is very popular in scrapbooking, and I thought it would make a fun card.

## The Giftcard Card

So many of us are giving giftcards these days...it's nice to have a fun and different way to deliver the present. This card is similar to the *Old Photos* card; however, it opens sideways. I added a small piece of the prepared fabric (see page 18) to the inside of the card, creating a pocket.

**Finished size:** $5'' \times 3\frac{1}{2}''$

**Pocket size:** $4\frac{1}{2}'' \times 2''$

### Supplies

Prepared fabric (see page 18)

Black, gold, and red cardstocks: Bazzill

Stencil letters: Li'l Davis Designs

1"-wide gold sheer ribbon

## Journey Card

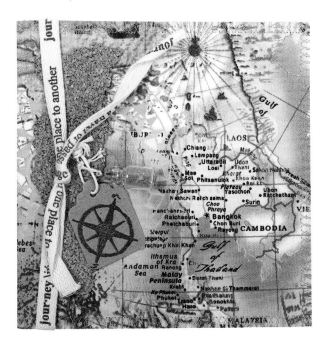

I love adding all kinds of charms and embellishments to my cards. If I were mailing this card, though, I would omit the small glass vial filled with sand for fear it would break en route. In keeping with the theme, it could be replaced with a charm of a plane or maybe a passport.

**Finished size:** *6"x 6"*

### Supplies

Prepared fabric (see page 18)

Cream cardstock

Journey twill tape: 7gypsies/Autumn Leaves

Kraft tag: American Tag

Compass stamp: Club Scrap

Rub-on letters: EK Success

Watch button: JHB

2 scraps thin cork paper

Small, brass safety pin

# HOLIDAY CARDS

Fun and beautiful greetings get anyone into the spirit!

## Witch Card

Premade die cuts are an easy way to create a fast greeting card. Available at your local scrapbook store, they come in all sorts of shapes, sizes, and themes. You can leave them plain or add some art glitter for pizzazz.

**Finished size:** $4\frac{3}{4}'' \times 6\frac{3}{4}''$

### Supplies

Prepared fabric (see page 18)

Black and two shades of orange cardstocks: Bazzill

Witch die cut

4 large black brads

# Joy Card

# Holly Card

**Finished size:** 7″ × 5″

## Supplies

Prepared fabric (see page 18)

Red, green, and cream cardstocks: Bazzill

Holiday background stamp: Hero Arts

Holly leaf stamp, embossed with gold embossing powder: A Stamp in the Hand

4 gold brads

This card opens up to an added treat of a matching holiday bookmark—the perfect little extra. This card would make a great teacher gift!

**Finished size:** 3¾″ × 8¼″

**Bookmark:** 2¼″ × 7″

## Supplies

Prepared fabric (see page 18)

Red, green, and light green cardstocks: Bazzill

Letter stickers: Provo Craft

Red tassel: Provo Craft

I left this card blank inside to add a photo or write my own greeting.

# LETTER CARDS

Sometimes when I make one of my fabric cards, I will add more pages inside the card so I can write a letter. The extra pages give me room for various options—a newspaper article, a photo, or even a drawing (in my case, a stamp) of what's going on in my life.

Here buttons and fibers add that finishing touch to a simple card.

The bricks are a perfect backdrop for the poster that my buddy Terrece made using a stamp from All Night Media.

# FABRIC JOURNALS

Sometimes a card just doesn't have enough space. So make a journal instead! You can make a card and add extra pages to it for journal entries, photos, recipes, or even fabric swatches from a special quilt.

There are a number of ways to attach the additional pages to the books. You can use a couple drops of glue to adhere a page or two inside a fabric cover, or…just follow these steps:

1. Cut several pages to fit inside your card.

2. Stack and layer the pages on a contrasting piece of cardstock.

3. Attach the pages to the cardstock with eyelets, brads, or rivets.

4. Attach the cardstock to the fabric card.

You can add fabric pages, too!

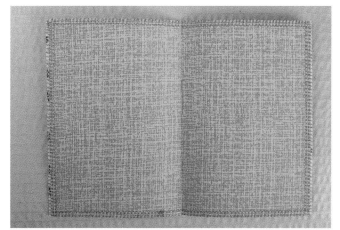

Sew them in!

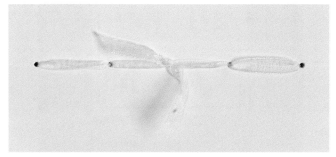

Drill holes along the spine and tie together with ribbon.

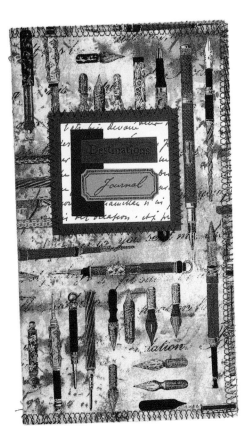

A super quick-and-easy travel journal to give as a gift or keep for yourself!

# Quilt Remembrance

I'm hooked on those antique and collectible shows that tell you what family heirlooms and treasures are worth. I especially get caught up in the dealers talking about the *provenance*, or history, of an item. Every time I look at my antique quilts, I wish I knew their story—where they came from, who made them, and what their life was like. Quilts are so much more than fabric, batting, and stitches; they are works of art from the heart.

This fabric journal provides the quilter a spot to tell the story of the quilt: why she made it, who helped, where she bought the fabric, what patterns she used, and what was going on in her life at that time. It also provides a spot for the person who received such a gift to describe what it means to her—

even if it's a gift from the quilter to herself! The journal can be attached to the quilt or kept in a pocket sewn to the back of the quilt.

**Finished size:** 4″ × 7¼″

## Supplies

(This supply list includes the materials I used for my entire journal, not just the page pictured)

Prepared fabric (see page 18), 4″ × 14½″

7 sheets of 3½″ × 13½″ paper (same as what you use as lining) folded in half. (I tore the short edges for a more vintage look.)

Old Paper Distress ink: Ranger Crafts

Alphabet stamps: Hero Arts

Sewing-related rubber stamps: Catslife Press, Postmodern Designs, Oxford Impressions

Permanent marker: Pigma Micron

Cording to tie the book together (I used a vintage shoelace.)

Assorted fabric scraps from the quilt

Scraps of assorted ribbons

Bits of embroidery thread

Sewing charms to decorate your pages

Vintage buttons

1. Layer your paper on top of your fabric cover.

2. With a screw punch, drill evenly spaced holes along the book's fold.

3. Tie the cover and pages together with cord or ribbon.

## TIP

All I could find at home was a white paper. It was a bit too bright, so I used a dye-based ink to give my paper an antique look. I love the results!

I made my first quilt remembrance journal about a quilt I created for C&T Publishing's *Photo Fun* book. I had such fun making it that I wanted a place to capture how special the quilt was to me.

I made sure to leave some extra pages at the back of the book to include the quilt's continuing story; quilt shows it may visit, classes it may get to instruct, walls it may grace.

A smaller book can be kept in a pocket stitched to the back of the quilt (remember to remove it before you wash the quilt). A larger book can be clipped to the quilt's display hanger.

## SEW MANY VARIATIONS!

I had so much fun playing with fabric covers that I went a little crazy in the studio. Here are some pictures of some fabric-covered books I created.

### The Story, the Photos

This book was pure fun. The story side has kraft-paper pages that have been roughed up a bit, and the photo side has black cardstock heavy enough to hold my pictures.

Recently my friend Terrece made her first quilt. When she saw the quilt storybook I made, she was again off to make her own version. The result was truly impressive! She made the trunk out of the prepared fabric and a paper booklet to tell the story of her first quilt.

## Wedding Guests

Create a guest book that matches the décor of the wedding! If you know someone who does calligraphy, have him or her make the pages or print them off your computer. For smaller weddings, you could also make a guest's program from matching fabric. What a special remembrance, or favor, to take home.

## Baby Advice

While this is intended for the baby-shower party guests to fill out during the party for a mom-to-be; it could also be created for a new bride, a new job, or reaching that magic age—whatever that may be!

## Fine Wine

I added lots of ribbons and some corks to complete the theme. I put small eyelet screws in the corks so I could tie them onto the spine of the book. You could make one about anything—postage stamps, email addresses, or even favorite songs. Find some related fabrics and embellishments, and you're good to go!

## The Four Seasons

I made this sleeve for a batik book set for a friend who likes to write poetry.

# Accordion Card

Here is one more variation of the card/book/gift. The fabric on this one is beautiful and came with several complementary fabrics. I thought it would be fun to replicate a paper book I'd seen, and the music fabric was perfect.

**Finished size:** 5″ × 6″

## TIP

Because this card is longer than my largest sheet of lining paper, I experimented with overlapping the lining paper a little, about ⅜″–½″. It worked perfectly. Now that the card is finished, I can't remember where the overlap is!

## Supplies

Prepared fabric (see page 18)

Gold, black, and cream cardstocks: Bazzill

¼″-wide sheer black and tan ribbons

Alphabet stamps: Stampotique Originals

Safety pin, *"sing,"* and metal corners: Making Memories

Assorted charms

Star and heart charm: JHB

Gold-leafing pen: Sakura Pen-touch

Black brads

Crochet cord

Wire ribbon

Vintage pearl button

# INVITATIONS

Have you seen all the food-related fabrics on the market today? So many fun and clever designs—wouldn't they make some wonderful invitations?! You can stamp the party information or print it directly onto cardstock from your computer.

## Come to My Party!

**Finished size:** 3⅞" × 11"; cut: 3⅞" × 8¾"

## Supplies

Prepared fabric (see page 18)

Black and white cardstocks: Bazzill

Hot Rod font: Creating Keepsakes Creative Lettering CD

⅜"-wide black sheer ribbon

## Wine Tasting, Anyone?

A friend gave me some leftover scraps of thin-cut cork (available at craft or home-improvement stores). It is wafer thin and easy to cut with scissors, a rotary cutter, or even a Sizzix machine (but handle it carefully, it is delicate). I thought it would make great texture for a greeting or invitation…and found it to be the perfect complement to this wine-tasting invitation!

**Finished size:** 6¾" × 5"

## Supplies

Prepared fabric (see page 18)

White cardstock: Bazzill

4 black brads: Lasting Impressions

Wine charms (found at a variety store)

6" × 4½"piece of thin cork

¾"-wide sheer wine-colored ribbon

### TIP

If you don't want to use your computer to print out your invitation, several stamp companies have blank invitation stamps available. Simply stamp it and fill in the particulars.

## A Cup of Joe?

When I saw this novelty print, I knew I could brew up a card featuring it!

## LITTLE EXTRAS

After cutting out my greeting cards, I will sometimes have some smaller scraps of prepared fabric left over. Here are some of the ways I have used up my scraps:

- For a recent trade show I made some business cards. I used my personal die cutter and the large-tag die cut. I printed a label out from my computer and sewed it directly to the tag. They were fun to do and were definitely memorable.

- You can also use the cut tags as a package gift tag. Print a to-from label on your computer (or stamp one!), sew or glue it to the tag, add a ribbon, and your gift is identified and ready to go!

- Bookmarks are another way to use up some of your fabric leftovers. They are great little extras to tuck into your card creations, include in a book you are giving, or make a whole bunch for boutique items. I usually cut my bookmarks based on the size of the leftover scrap. Sometimes, if

the bookmark is a gift, I will let the fabric design guide me. That can cause a bit more waste, but if I really like the design, it's worth it!

I try to have some of these quick and easy extras on hand, so when I need one I'm ready!

You can also fussy cut complete images from your scraps and use them as embellishments for quick cards.

# Machine care for sewing on paper:

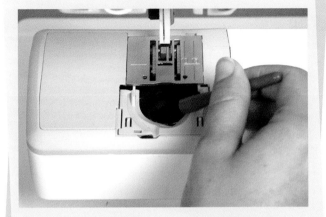

■ Clean your machine of any dust and lint particles often.

■ If you hear a small popping sound while sewing the edges of your card (paper) or your machine starts skipping stitches, it may be time to change your needle. Paper will dull your sewing machine needle much faster than fabric.

## TIP

Use a small dab of a glue stick or tape in the center of the wrong side of the cardstock to prevent it from shifting while sewing it to a fabric card. Be sure not to put glue where you will be sewing!

## TIP

Leaving clipped threads showing has become a popular trend with card and scrapbook enthusiasts. Try a couple of cards both ways to decide which look you like best.

# Game Board Cards

Family Album by Margaret Rogers

As a collector of "treasures," I buy lots of old board games for use in various art projects and scrapbook quilts. From these games, I was using only the playing cards, pieces, dice, and tiles. That left lots of actual game boards stacking up around the studio. I couldn't part with them, and knew there had to be a way to put them to good use. They are sturdy and fold up nicely just like a card...a *card*! It was, as they say, "a light bulb moment." Because this idea came to me on the heels of the fabric cards, I had already ironed lots of fabric adhesive to fabric. I got to thinking that I could cut a larger piece of prepared fabric to iron on the outside of the board and decorate the inside with paper, photos, and embellishments, creating a mega-size greeting card.

Game boards come in all sizes!

# STARTING OUT

After some experimentation, I finally came up with the following set of instructions for a basic game board card. The hardest thing to do is decide on a theme!

# BASIC SUPPLIES

Game board

Fabric (enough to cover the outside of the game board)

Acrylic paint and a paintbrush or small paint roller

Fabric adhesive

Iron and ironing board

Rotary cutter

Cutting mat

Clear acrylic ruler

1. Prepare the board by painting the outside edges and center of the inside of the game board.

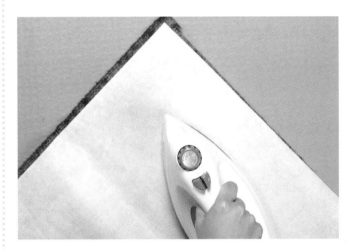

2. When cutting your fabric, measure the height and width of the open game board. Trim your fabric to the height *minus* ½" and to the width *plus* 1". With a dry iron fuse fabric adhesive to the wrong side of the fabric.

3. Carefully place your cut fabric ¼" in from the edge of the game board for a smooth, finished look. Iron the fabric onto one side of the game board.

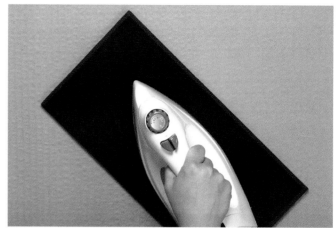

4. By leaving a bit of extra fabric on the width of the game board, you ensure having a piece large enough to evenly cover the back of the board. Trim fabric to measure to within ⅛" of the edge of the board.

6. Iron the remaining side of the game board. From here you are ready to decorate your card for whatever occasion you may need.

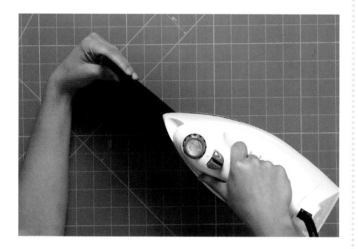

## TIP

If I want to finish off the inside of the game board with decorative paper, I paint only the center crease of the board (as shown) in the first step of this project. I then trim the paper to come within ½" of both sides and the center of the game board. This helps to keep my finished card as flat as possible. If I have a very sturdy game board, I can paint the entire background, then decorate with my selected embellishments. If the game board is thin or flimsy, painting the entire board will cause it to warp and not stand on its own.

5. Iron the remaining fabric to the spine.

A game board makes a great base for other related art projects. You can decorate it to match a room, become a message board, become a remembrance of someone special to you, or other item you may want to make. If you want more ideas, check out decorating and scrapbook magazines. They provide great examples of style, color use, and how to pull it all together. Even furniture and gift catalogs can be great inspiration.

# BIRTHDAYS
## Big Birthday

A great big birthday card for friends or family that you can make in minutes!

### Supplies

Small game board

Prepared fabric (see page 43)

Purple metallic paint: Lumiere

Two sheets each of two graduating shades of purple cardstocks: Bazzill

Foam alphabet stamps: Making Memories

Green and purple paper circles in 3 or 4 assorted sizes: Sizzix die cuts

1¼"-wide decorative ribbon

Black acrylic paint

## Happy Birthday, Happy Birthday

This one is all fun and colors! I covered the game board with black paint and then color-blocked the inside as frames for my message. Now it's time to really put that Sizzix machine to work! I purchased an alphabet die set and borrowed another from a friend to come up with this *Happy Birthday, Happy Birthday* card.

The party hat was made from a triangle, small star, and circles from a medium-size hole punch.

## TIP

Covering the inside of a game board takes a large piece of cardstock. Art stores usually carry large sizes, but if you can't get to the art store, you can use a couple of 12" × 12" pieces of cardstock instead. Select your main color and cut two pieces of cardstock the width of the inside of the game board. Then, cut smaller accent pieces of a complementary color to cover the ends of the board.

See how the complementary purple adds to an overall simple design?

## Supplies

- Small game board
- Prepared fabric (see page 43)
- Ready-made birthday cake: Paper Bliss
- Nine complementary colors of cardstocks: Colormates
- Letters to spell out your wishes: Sizzix diecuts
- Geometric shapes to frame some of the words: Sizzix die cuts or hole punches
- Happy Birthday stamp: Hero Arts
- Heart paper punch: EK Success
- Black eyelets

# MORE IDEAS
## She Can Fly

This was my first attempt at an "artsy"-looking game board. I just fell in love with the paper-doll image and the size of the game board was perfect as her backdrop. She looks a bit forlorn, as if she wants to fly…like she can in her dreams.

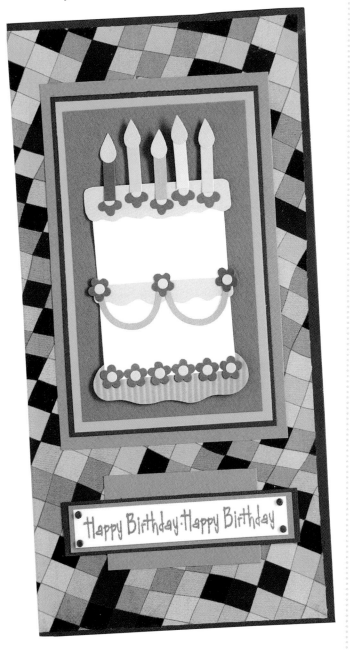

## Supplies

Large game board

Prepared fabric to cover game board (see page 43)

Prepared script fabric (see page 43)

Black, cream, and ivory cardstocks: Petersen-Arne

Large sheet cream paper cut to fit inside of game board: Canson

Paper doll: Invoke Arts

Metal decorative corners: K&Company

Gold butterfly scrap: Rubber Baby Buggy Bumpers

Doll wings (two sizes painted with gold metallic paint)

Metal letter tiles in assorted sizes: Making Memories

Woven word label: Me & My Big Ideas

Gold leafing to highlight edges of game board: Amy's Magic

Large alphabet stamps: Ma Vinci's Reliquary

Crown charm

Postage stamps

## NOTE

I stamped my alphabet, cut the letters out, and then painted them to match the vintage look I wanted.

## Art

I love the fabric I used to cover the game board—it called out to have some artistic diva live inside. She is one of my muses and creative spirits. She provides encouragement, reminding me to branch out, even if it's just a little bit!

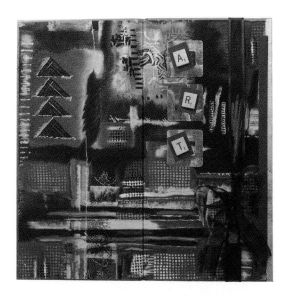

## Supplies

Small game board

Prepared fabric (see page 43)

Gold cord and tassel: Provo Craft

Metal letters: Making Memories

Metal inspirational words: Making Memories

Acrylic Slide frame: Heidi Grace Designs

Party hat: Deluxe Cuts

"Wonder" (from an old label maker)

Red perle cotton: DMC

Stamps:

Dice, Ticket, Bingo Card, Legs: Fusion Art Stamps

Artsy: Stampotique Originals

"Imagine": Catslife Press

"Expect", "Envision", "Home", "Dream": River City Rubber Works

Face: Zettiology

Arms: Limited Edition

Hand: Stamp in the Hand

Lips: JudiKins

Vintage slide mounts (I found these at a garage sale!)

Vintage game tiles

Domino

"Ace" game tile

Small game chip

Words "eye" and "can" from a vintage learning set

Optical lens (I got the idea to crack the lens from Tim Holtz—love the results!)

1½ yards 1"-wide sheer black ribbon

Black acrylic paint

Gold metallic paint

# MORE IDEAS
## Wedding Card

I found a smaller, almost-square game board and was intrigued by its size. I started playing around, and it became this beautiful wedding card. It could easily be transformed into a special anniversary card—just add a little more gold or silver as your accent.

## Supplies

Small game board

Prepared fabric (see page 43)

Cream, tan, and taupe cardstocks

Heart stamp: Stampington

Textured mulberry bark (I raided a friend's treasure stash for this white mesh!)

Gold-leafing pen: Krylon

Vintage buttons

Ribbon and lace scraps

Metal photo corners: ProvoCraft

## Wedding Invitation

A friend was having a small, intimate wedding ceremony and wanted very special invitations for her guests. This unique card created by Krista Halligan is the result!

## Hooray for Retirement!

I wanted to try working on a game board that wasn't covered with fabric. I painted the entire board metallic silver and used black cardstock as my backdrop for the letters and a very special picture. Inside I attached an pocket and stuffed it with "idea tags" full of ways to spend newfound spare time.

### Supplies

Small game board

Shiny black, white, and three shades of purple cardstocks: Bazzill

Black script-printed paper: DMD

Alphabet rubber stamps: Wordsworth

White metal frame: Paper Parachute

Vellum heart tag: Making Memories

Inspirational word rubber stamps: Jody Poesy

Heart pearl button: JHB

Embossing ink

Silver embossing powder

1½"-wide decorative ribbon

Vintage shiny black letters

Vintage black twill tape

⅛"-wide ribbon

Silver eyelets

Silver metallic paint

### TIP

This layout would make a great graduation card, too. Just add the graduate's picture on the front of the card; the family can put their best wishes on the tags in the envelope.

## Teacher Appreciation

I've noticed a lot of teachers using scrapbooking as a way to teach kids about themselves. I thought up this game board idea as a way for the students to give a little something back to their teacher.

*Tags in the "Free Time" Pocket*

Scraps of paper in complementary colors

Assorted letters: EK Success, Making Memories, Colorbök, Creative Imaginations

Snippets of ribbon

Assorted "free-time related" charms

Life stickpin: K&Company

Laminate sample tile

Doll wings (painted metallic purple)

## Supplies

Large game board

Prepared fabric (see page 43)

Red, orange, yellow, green, and black cardstocks: Bazzill

Letters: Sizzix die cuts

School writing paper: Making Memories

Ruler ribbon, ³⁄₈"-wide black-and-white mini-check ribbon, ¹⁄₄"-wide satin ribbon: Offray

Chalkboard button: JHB

Tags

Kids and schoolhouse charms (Mine came from a garage sale necklace!)

Photos of kids

Black acrylic paint

## TIP

I didn't have a piece of cardstock long enough for the red cardstock ribbon on the front of the board, so I simply cut two smaller pieces and tucked them under the yellow cardstock. I used what I had and no one knows my secret…shhhh!

## Mom's Board

My mom loves anything to do with nature (except for lizards!). I try to make all her cards with images of flowers, leaves, birds, and bees. The images are fun to collect and getting some of the supplies is as easy as taking a walk outside. After carefully wrapping the twig with wire, I found that The Ultimate! glue worked perfectly to attach the wrapped twig to the card.

## Supplies

Small game board

Prepared fabric (see page 43)

Paper (I painted this with Lumiere paints)

Cream textured cardstock for inside of board: Canson

Mini metal fern plaque: Making Memories

Bee buttons: JHB

Kraft tags: American Tag

Silver hinges: FoofaLa

Cork tags: Creative Imaginations

Metal screening: Making Memories

Ruler and label holder sticker: EK Success

Glass leaf embellishments: Stamper's Warehouse

Keyhole stickpin: K&Company

Old trading card images

Old watch face

Vintage sheet music

Vintage pearl buttons

Vintage hatpin (I found this at a flea market.)

Vintage letter "B"

"Mom" letters: Creative Imaginations

Small beading pin

Gold skeleton leaf

Glassine coin envelope

Eyelets

Assorted torn pages from old books

Plant tag

Preserved leaf scrap (Leaves from fake plants would work just as well!)

Found feathers, acorn caps, and a twig

¾"-wide sheer ribbon

Gold wire

Green metallic paint

## Girl Power

I really thought the shape of this game board was interesting and would make a fun display. I went with a retro theme and decided to showcase some of my favorite girly girls!

### Supplies

Prepared fabric (see page 43)

Pink, light yellow, and blue cardstocks: Colormates

Pink flower decorated paper: KI Memories

Flower stamp: Making Memories

Alphabet stamps: Hero Arts

2004 stickers: Provo Craft

Assorted tags: Sizzix die cuts

Assorted ribbons and fibers

Silver curly paper clip

Yellow mini clothespin

Pink and hot pink acrylic paint

# Vintage Collection

One day I started pulling my favorite treasures out to make a game board—not so much for a card, but for a showcase of my loves and treasured collections. Here is the result, definitely a keeper!

## Supplies

Large game board

Prepared fabric (This time I used crumpled kraft paper as my "fabric." See pages 10 and 43.)

Black, cream, tan, and kraft cardstocks

Printed woven text: Creative Imaginations

Script and alphabet paper: 7gypsies

Scrap of thin cork paper

Burnt sienna colorwash (I used this over the printed papers and the cork to age them a bit.): Golden

Decorated eyelets, printed twill tape: Making Memories

Key, black lace: EK Success

Metal letters, oval label holder, and washer: Making Memories

Dress form diecut: Limited Edition

"Fragile" dog tag: Poetry Dog Tags

Crown and small compass charms

Green crown seal: Marcel Shurman

Thimble, scissors, and sewing machine charms and button stickpin: K&Company

Stamps:

Woman collage, words: Stampotique

"Misunderstood", button-card: Paper Bag Studios

Pattern: B Line Designs

Lotto wheel: Invoke Arts

Alphabet: Ma Vinci's Reliquary

Face (embossed with gold embossing powder): Zettiology

Snaps in assorted sizes

1¼"-wide black-and-tan checked, wired ribbon

Vintage ¼"-wide olive green twill tape

¾"-wide vintage rickrack

Old doily (I found this one at a garage sale for 25¢!)

Used ticket stub

Bingo card

Scraps of assorted ribbon, wire, fabric, tulle, and vintage paper

Vintage photo

Vintage Q stencil

Vintage sheet music

Vintage black and pearl buttons in assorted sizes

Piece of broken ruler

Watch face

Embroidery thread

# HOLIDAYS
## Fourth of July

While cleaning out some art supplies recently, I came across a basket of red, white, and blue treasures I had collected for a friend's birthday card. I put the basket on my worktable, right next to a game board. That's all it took to get me started!

## TIP

The scrapbook companies have many products available relating to military service. Wouldn't this board be great as a welcome home for a soldier?

## Supplies

Large game board

Prepared fabrics (see page 43)

Red and blue cardstocks: Canson

*America* printed sheet music: DMD

Alphabet stamps: Making Memories, Hero Arts

"Liberty" and large star buttons: JHB

Red frames: Li'l Davis Designs

Red printed twill tape: Making Memories

Cream perle cotton thread: DMC

Metal letter tiles in assorted sizes: Making Memories

Metal dog tags: Li'l Davis Designs

Metal star button

Small flag

Vintage tag

Vintage photo of woman enlarged to fit game board

Vintage photo of dog

Vintage flag

Vintage red buckle

Vintage *United States Lines* game piece and flag scrap

Vintage large *P* stencil

½"-wide sheer red ribbon

White and blue acrylic paints

## TIP

I had fun playing with fabric on this board. I used the red-stripe fabric as the base and then added a strip of blue-star fabric around the outside fold.

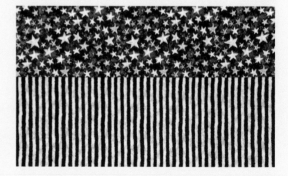

# Twelve Days of Christmas

For a few years my friend and I have made the "Twelve Days of Christmas" an event (well, twelve events, actually). On each of the twelve days before Christmas we give each other a little treat. (Yes, we're a little spoiled!) It's like getting our Christmas stocking gifts spread out over a number of days. Over the years, the gifts have gotten smaller because it isn't about the gift, it's about remembering a special event or just making each other smile. This board is a way to continue our tradition but to make it more personal, homemade, and meaningful. The pockets are numbered and can hold a poem, a giftcard from your favorite store or restaurant, old postcards, a favorite photograph, paper dolls (all decked out for the holidays!), movie passes, a recipe with a promise to make it, or coupons (like one for getting out of washing the dishes!). I wonder how my favorite candy will fit into the pockets?

## Supplies

Large game board

Prepared fabric (see page 43)

Green, dark green, black, tan, red cardstocks (I randomly cut pockets from the cardstock and sewed them together, except where a specific design is listed.):

Bazzill

Large harlequin stamp: Postmodern Design

Versamark inkpad: Tsukiniko

Large sheet of black paper to line the inside: Strathmore

Gold metal "paper" (I put mine through the crimping tool to create some texture.): EK Success

Gold metal frames, bar, and metal corners: EK Success

Stencil letters: Li'l Davis Designs

Assorted foam stamp alphabet letters: Making Memories

Vintage game letter tiles

Number 12 from a vintage game card

Green acrylic paint for letters on the front

Gold acrylic paint for highlights on the inside paper

## Pocket Supplies

**One**

Merry Christmas ribbon: Making Memories

Gold brad: Lasting Impressions

Vintage number 1

**Two**

Number 2 stamp: Stamper's Anonymous

Vintage black seam binding

**Three**

Vintage number 3 plastic house number

Thin gold wire

**Four**

Music paper: Penny Black

Black diamond paper (I also used green color wash to give this paper a light green tint.): 7gypsies.

Metal letters: Making Memories

Metal "love" tag: Marcella by Kay

Green tassel: Provo Craft

Number 4 from a vintage flash card

Pearl button

Vintage key

Green ribbon scrap

**Five**

Green fiber adornments: EK Success

Black tag and number 5 rub-on transfer: Making Memories

Vintage keyhole

**Six**

Metal arrow

"Made with love" twill tape: 7gypsies

Decorative metal strip (I painted mine cream, let it dry, then lightly added some green paint on the ridges with a dry brush.): Making Memories

Large-print stamp: Postmodern Design

Number 6 plastic house number (Again I painted the number cream, then dry-brushed green paint over it.)

### TIP

You could adapt this game board into an advent calendar. Make sure you get a very large game board and make your 24 pockets smaller—there are lots of great envelope and pocket templates to help you. Too much work? Have a calendar-making party. Get together with friends to make the calendar and ask everyone to bring enough of the same handmade treasure to fill one envelope for each guest. Your calendar will be filled in no time. How festive... wouldn't this make a great gift for newlyweds or baby's first Christmas?

**Seven**

Gold metal frame: EK Success

Crown charm

Number 7 from metal and foam alphabet: Making Memories

Red-ribbon adornment: EK Success

Scrap of diamond paper (tinted with green wash): 7gypsies

Large-script stamps: Postmodern Design

6 gold eyelets

**Eight**

Number 8 from a plastic alphabet set (found at a dollar store)

String tie closure: EK Success

**Nine**

 Envelope: pattern from Deluxe Cuts

 Vintage number *9* (I painted this with cream-colored acrylic paint.)

 Black brads: Lasting Impressions

 Metal words: Making Memories

 Metal stamp square: FoofaLa

 Pear charm

 Laminated tag

**Ten**

 Red fiber adornments: EK Success

 Metal-rimmed tag and silver frame: Making Memories

 Number *10* stickers: Provo Craft

 Red heart charm: JHB

 11 square silver brads

**Eleven**

 Metal tree tile: Making Memories

 Red perle cotton: DMC

 Flat spring: 7gypsies

 Gold frame: EK Success

 Scrap of diamond paper (tinted with green wash): 7gypsies

 Assorted charms

 Metal "Celebrate": Making Memories

 Assorted ribbon scraps

 Vintage slide mount painted black

 Number *11* from old playing cards

**Twelve**

 Decorative paper: Penny Black and Bo Bunny Press

 Two black tabs: 7gypsies

 Number *12* stamp: Stampotique Originals

 Two black brads: Lasting Impressions

 Fun silver heart

# STARTING OUT

Now, if you don't have time to prepare fabric for a fabric or game board card, you can still whip up some terrific greetings with some of the same supplies you already have on hand—cardstock, decorative paper, and embellishments. Throw in a couple of stamped images and you're ready to make some cards!

# BIRTHDAYS

## 29 Again?

When this dog diecut came into the store I laughed all day. He just made me smile. I knew he would make a perfect birthday card! This one is all about layering the beautiful colors on top of each other. I generally leave about ¼" showing on each side of the layers—but more or less on different layers—which adds interest.

**Finished size:** 5" × 7"

## Supplies

   Green, black, and medium and dark purple cardstocks: (Bazzill)

   Dog die cut: Meri Meri Accents

   Number and question mark 29?: Sizzix diecuts

## Birthday Pocket

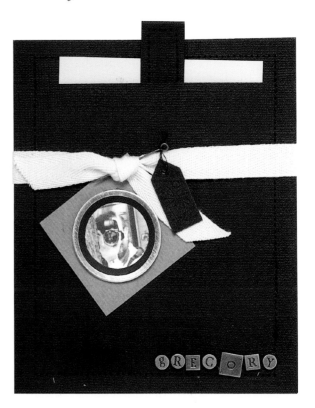

I have fun making tags. Sometimes I make the tag, and then need to figure out how to give it to the person. In this case, the tag was a simple happy birthday wish. That's what happened with this card—I started out with a collage tag, then I created the pocket for it.

**Finished sizes:**

**Pocket:** 4¾" × 5¾"

**Tag:** 3⅜" × 5"

## Supplies

   Black, tan, red, and gold cardstocks

   Matte black brad: Lasting Impressions

   Metal letters and black metal-rimmed tag: Making Memories

   Tag, square, and circle punches: EK Success

   Stickpin: Making Memories

   Twill tape

## To Make a Pocket

**1.** Cut two pieces of cardstock the size of the tag plus ½" on each side and ¼" on the top and bottom.

**2.** Cut 1–1¼" away on one side of the pocket, line up the two pieces of cardstock, and sew about ¼" in on each side and the bottom.

Presto! You have a pocket!

## Clown Surprise

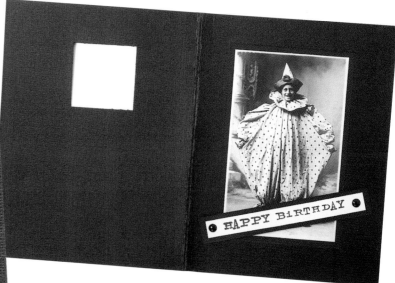

### HAPPY BiRTHDAY

This is a super simple card using an old photo that hides behind the front of the card. Use a handheld square hole punch to punch the window on your card, then use it again on a piece of black cardstock. Trim the black ¼" away from the edge of the window with decorative-edge scissors, and you have a frame.

**Finished size:** 4¼" × 5½"

### Supplies

Red, black, and cream cardstocks: Bazzill

Happy Birthday stamp: Catslife Press

2 black brads: Lasting Impressions

Alphabet stamp: Hero Arts

Square hole punch: Whale of a Punch—EK Success

Small circle punch: EK Success

Decorative-edge scissors

Old photo

# MORE IDEAS
## Hugs & Kisses

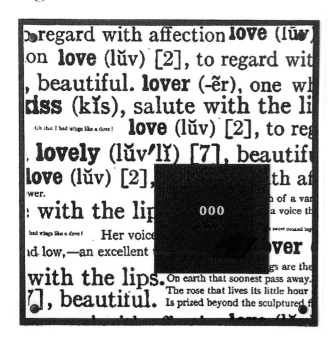

I really like working with the colors black, red, and white. When I found these labels, I immediately saw the finished card in my head.

**Finished size:** *6" × 6"*

## Supplies

Black, red, and white cardstocks: Bazzill

Love acetate: 7gypsies

Acrylic lips: Heidi Grace Designs

Fabric labels: Threads by Me & My Big Ideas

4 black brads

Vintage black seam binding

## Hands

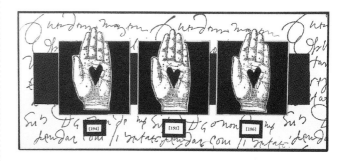

A fun, graphic card using my favorite colors, again!

**Finished size:** *8¾" × 3¾"*

## Supplies

Black, red, and cream cardstocks: Bazzill

Small heart punch: EK Success

Hand stamp, script stamp: A Stamp in the Hand

Page numbers from vintage books

Gold-leaf pen: Krylon

## Hope

While I was cleaning up the studio after a card-making marathon, I came across the word "hope" and the green cardstock. I started playing around, and this is the result. Playing is so much more fun than cleaning!

**Finished size:** *9¾" × 3¾"*

## Supplies

Dark and light green cardstocks

"Hope" (This time I painted the word with a couple coats of cream-colored acrylic paint.): Making Memories

Circle medallion (I "antiqued" this by brushing on some burnt umber acrylic paint then wiping off the excess.): EK Success

Fern stamp: Hero Arts

Gold embossing powder and embossing ink

Gold-leaf pen: Krylon

¼"-wide sheer ribbon

# JUST FOR LAUGHS

So many wonderful sayings are available in rubber stamps, and these made me howl with laughter. It is good to have a few of these stamps in your tool kit—whether it produces a giggle from the person who is lucky enough to get a hand-made card, or it cheers you while you make the card!

## If I Have to Wear Pantyhose

Finished size: 5" × 7"

## *Supplies*

Black, gold, and olive green cardstocks

Script paper: DMD

*"If I Have to Wear Pantyhose"* stamp: Rubbermoon

Old photo

Vintage pearl buttons

Snippet of ribbon in a complementary color

## Pretending to Be Normal

Finished size: 5" x 7"

## *Supplies*

Olive green cardstock

Olive print paper

*"Pretending to be Normal"* stamp: River City Rubber Works

Old photo

# HOLIDAYS
## Happy Halloween

Halloween is probably my favorite holiday. I decorate the house, buy lots of pumpkins, and try to make at least a couple of cards to send out to friends. When I found these buttons I knew I had to get into the studio to make these…for me!

**Finished size:** 3¾" × 9¾"

## Supplies

Black, gold, and rust cardstocks

Two cat and two pumpkin buttons: Just Another Button Company

## Jack O' Lantern

Isn't he the best?

**Finished size:** 4" × 5½"

## Supplies

Black, gold, rust, and cream cardstocks: Bazzill

Black mesh: Making Memories

¼"-wide black polka-dot grosgrain ribbon

*"Jack"* stamp: Just for Fun

*"Trick or Treat"* stamp: Hero Arts

Black ink: Marvey

# Christmas

I can spend hours making a card for various occasions throughout the year. At Christmas, because so many of my gifts are handmade, the cards are usually fast and easy!

## Ho³ Card

**Finished size:** *3" × 6"*

### Supplies

Red and green cardstocks: Bazzill

Metal letters: Colorbök

Metal number 3: Making Memories

¼"-wide red mini-check ribbon: Offray

**TIP**

The insides of both cards are blank, for now. I will fill each one with holiday sentiment, once I know to whom the card is going.

## A Merry Card

**Finished size:** *6" × 3¼"*

### Supplies

Red and 3 shades of green cardstocks: Bazzill

White card base: Hero Arts

¼"-wide red mini-check ribbon: Offray

Metal letters: Colorbök

# Love & Joy

Santa peeks out of the top of the pocket because he can't wait to wish everyone a Merry Christmas! I used a color photocopy of a vintage Santa postcard as the cover. You could make this card in any theme using a color copy of a vintage photo or postcard.

**Finished sizes:**

**Card:** 5¼" × 7

**Pocket:** 3⅝" × 5½"

## Supplies

Red and green cardstocks: Bazzill

Metal "love" and &: Making Memories

Metal frame: 7gypsies

24" of 1"-wide, green satin ribbon

Alphabet stamps: Postmodern Design

Wooden number 25

Black crochet cotton

Red metal frame: Magic Scraps

# PAPER DOLLS

I just loved playing with paper dolls when I was a kid. I still have one of the sets that came from a coloring book I got on a visit to my grandparents in Pennsylvania. It was so much fun coloring in the clothes the way I thought they should be done! Recently, when I started seeing all the art paper dolls people were creating I knew I had to get into the act. I stamp up a bunch of dolls on various colors of cardstock all at one time, cut them out while watching movies, and store them in an old film can till they are ready to come out and play. Making paper dolls this way saves me time and gives me lots of options when I want to start creating. I like to select a theme for my dolls and use related background stamps to fill in the legs, arms, body, or hats...whatever strikes my fancy. It's fun to look through your stash of stamps to see what you might be able to create!

## Stamping Diva
**Finished size:** 3¾″ × 8¾″

## Supplies

Red, yellow, and black cardstocks: Bazzill

Decorative graph paper

Medium heart punch: EK Success

Japanese screw punch (to make small holes for brads)

Doll head, art ink stamps: A Stamp in the Hand

Paint brushes stamps: Sunday International

Square alphabet stamps: Leavenworth Jackson

Small hat stamp

Background for legs stamp

4 black brads

## Queen of Buttons

Both of these cards were inspired for my love of sewing-related treasures. I am mad for pearl buttons, and the sew mistress one was inspired by a child's vintage sewing machine.

## Sew Mistress

## Jack Halloween

Collecting vintage Halloween is very popular and, thanks to Mom, I'm lucky enough to have a few old pumpkin candy containers myself. I made this Halloween doll with those decorations in mind. The "jack" head stamp was a perfect fit over the paper doll. I added a few small circle punched embellishments and a crown hat—he was ready to go to the party!

## Be True

This one was made as a sample for the store where I work. The challenge was to use some of the popular metal tags we had in stock. I decided to add some of my favorite things—old photos, crowns, paper dolls, and a heart—for a stylish result.

# IN A HURRY?

Here are some helpful ideas for those occasions on which you say, "Help! I need a card, quick!" When I make cards I usually start by creating a number of bases and gathering a bunch of elements. This allows me to try different compositions before I settle on just the right one. When I have completed the original project, I will store the leftover stamped images, words, and extra letters with similar images, so when I need a card quick, I have some stock to pull from.

## Batik Card Bases

Batik card bases are a great way to have some fun, ready-to-go stock on hand. Batiks come in wonderful colors, and the different colors and patterns seem to lend themselves to a variety of card-giving occasions.

Simply prepare some fabric as shown on page 18, make a few of them and you'll always have one on hand for that last-minute card.

## Card Templates

Another option is to use one of the many card templates that are available today. Fun shapes paired up with a decorative paper and a neat stamp make for a fast, fun, and easy card.

### TIP

When I make a card to send to a friend, I try to remember to make a photocopy of it. By doing this, I have a record of what cards I sent out. But more important, I have a pattern to follow when I want to make another one in a hurry!

## Tag, You're It!

Okay, so you don't have a lot of time and you're short on ideas. What about a tag greeting? All you have to do is select a couple colors of cardstock, and stamp some letters. Put the tags together and thread the tags onto some ribbon—I like to use vintage seam binding. Place the greeting in a fun-shaped envelope, and you're good to go!

# Finishing Up

its party time

please come!

# SIGNING YOUR CARDS

After putting all that work into your greeting cards, don't forget to sign the back of your creation! It can be a simple date and signature, or you can use some leftover elements from the front of the card with your signature or you can get one of the many rubber stamps available to simply stamp on the back of the card. Whatever you do, just sign it. Your art is important because it is from you.

# ENVELOPES

Now that you have all these great cards made, it's time to mail some to your friends. To be able to send them, you will need some envelopes. I made most of the fabric and paper cards to fit into standard-size envelopes. You can find envelopes in all types of stores: scrapbook stores, stationers, office supply stores, grocery stores, and even the post office.

Here is a chart of some basic sizes:

| Envelope code | Size |
| --- | --- |
| Baronial | $3/8'' \times 5''$ |
| A-2 | $4^3/8'' \times 5^3/4''$ |
| A-6 | $4^3/4'' \times 6^1/2''$ |
| A-7 | $5^1/4'' \times 7^1/2''$ |
| A-8 | $5^1/2'' \times 8^1/8''$ |
| A-10 | $6'' \times 9^1/2''$ |
| #10 (Business size) | $4^1/8'' \times 9^1/2''$ |

## TIP

While envelopes do come in various sizes and colors, the easiest and most inexpensive envelope to find is usually a plain white one. Decorating your plain envelope is another way to add some pizzazz. You can add various colors of ink, paint, stamps, or even fabric appliqués for a fun, one-of-a-kind look. Just make sure to leave enough visible room for legible mailing and return addresses!

You could also try using a see-through or cellophane envelope, available at most rubber stamp stores. These allow the recipient to see the card inside. If you don't want them to see the whole card yet, include some cut tissue paper in the envelope. They are easy to use—just place an address sticker on the front and the appropriate postage, and it is set to mail.

Vellum envelopes are another option. These are beautiful but a bit pricier and a bit more difficult to find. Because of the nature of vellum, these envelopes are another way to reveal the card a bit, without giving the whole design away.

Making envelopes is probably the most fun, though. There are so many wonderful templates on the market today that make it really easy. The templates are geared to standard-size cards and are usually very easy to use. To match your card creation, you can purchase "new" paper for your envelope or you can use old magazines, calendars, wrapping paper, wallpaper, or even maps…basically anything large enough to fit the template.

## Making Your Own

So your artistic side got ahead of your practical side—you just finished a great card, but it doesn't fit into a standard-size envelope. What to do? Here are some directions for creating an envelope in no time to fit your card perfectly. These instructions will allow you to make an envelope to fit any size card—as long as you have a piece of paper large enough. I have used a 12″ × 12″ piece of paper for the example.

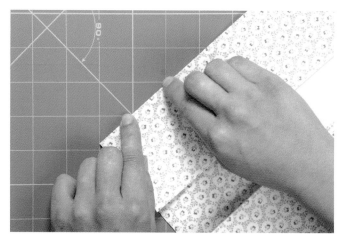

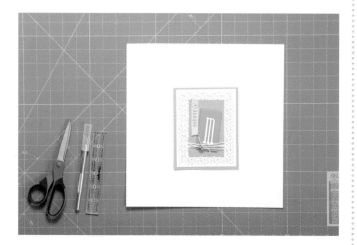

1. Take your card and lay it on a large sheet of paper.

2. Fold the bottom of the paper up to cover two-thirds of your card. Crease with a bone folder.

3. Fold in the sides of the envelope paper to within ⅛″ of each side of the card.

4. Unfold and cut away the excess (corners) along each side. After the excess is trimmed away, trim the sides to 1″. Refold the envelope.

5. You may need to trim at a slight angle along the bottom and top flaps to ensure a finished look.

Spectacular Cards

6. Fold down and glue the flap in place.

For a larger card, you will need a larger piece of paper. Here are some rough measurements to help you calculate what your paper size will need to be:

1. For your base, use the card measurement.

2. Add 2½" to the width measurement.

3. Double the height measurement and add 1" for the top and bottom flaps.

So if you have a card that is 7½" × 8½", you would need a piece of paper that is at least 11" × 18" for the handmade envelope.

NOTE

One of the most popular card sizes today is the 6" × 6". It's a different, fun size and has lots of room to decorate or collage. The only frustration is that it requires more postage because the post office doesn't consider the shape a standard size. You can remedy this by using a larger, standard-size envelope.

# SENDING YOUR CARDS

I have found it to be in bad form to send a greeting card with postage due! Fabric cards do typically weigh a bit more. By the time I add a few embellishments, I need a couple postage stamps on them. To save trips to the post office each time I send a card, I have a small postage scale to find the weight of the card. I then check the United States Postal Service's website (www.usps.com) to find the postage it will require. Remember to read all the fine print, and make sure you follow all the rules and size constraints. If you have added a lot of embellishments and are worried about your card arriving safely, consider having the envelope hand canceled, adding some thin cardboard to the inside of the envelope, or sending your greeting in a larger, padded envelope. The padded envelope may cost more to mail, but your beautiful artwork will be protected.

As for shipping game board cards, I try to keep the original boxes that came with the game for easy giving or mailing. The decorated board still fits perfectly and can be easily wrapped. I usually take these packages directly to the post office for mailing.

As a final thought, keep your card creations in perspective. I send handmade creations to those individuals who will truly appreciate the card and give my small works of art the appropriate attention and respect they deserve. One of my friends has placed all the cards I have sent him on a shelf in his hall. He lovingly refers to them as the "shrine." This is definitely considered showing appropriate respect!

Happy creating!

# SOURCES

Special thanks to the following companies for supplying products used in the book:

**The Crafter's Pick**: "The Ultimate!" glue www.crafterspick.com

**EK Success**: lots of embellishments, metallic papers, and fibers www.eksuccess.com

**Hoffman California Fabrics**: beautiful Christmas fabrics www.hoffmanfabrics.com

**JHB Buttons**: novelty buttons and charms www.buttons.com

**Just Another Button Company**: Halloween pumpkins and cats www.justanotherbuttoncompany.com

**Lakehouse Designs**: fabric with a vintage feel

**Ranger Crafts**: Nonstick craft sheets, inks, and colorwashes. www.rangerink.com

**Sizzix**: personal die-cut machines, dies, and other accessories www.sizzix.com

**Therm O Web**: HeatnBond UltraHold Iron-On Adhesive www.thermoweb.com

**Timeless Treasures**: wonderful novelty and batik fabrics www.hi-fashionfabrics.com

*Some of these companies only sell wholesale, but most of the websites list where to buy the products retail.*

# STAMP COMPANIES

**All Night Media, Inc.**
www.allnightmedia.com/apANM.asp

**B Line Designs**
1212 E Kay
Mustang, OK 73064
405.376.3351

**Catslife Press**
www.harborside.com/~catslife

**The Cat's Pajamas Rubber Stamps**
www.thecatspajamasrs.com

**Club Scrap**
www.clubscrap.com

**Fusion Art Stamps**
www.fusionartstamps.com

**Hampton Art Stamps**
www.hamptonart.com

**Hero Arts**
www.heroarts.com

**Invoke Arts**
www.invokearts.com

**Jody Poesy Rubber Art Stamps**
www.jodypoesy.com

**JudiKins**
www.judikins.com

**Junque**
www.junque.net

**Just for Fun Rubber Stamps**
www.jffstamps.com

**Leavenworth Jackson Rubber Stamps**
www.ljackson.com

**Limited Edition Rubber Stamps**
www.limitededitionrs.com

**Lost Coast Designs**
www.lost-coast-designs.com

**Love to Stamp**
*Write and ask for a catalog:*
3131 Dellrose Rd. SW
Tumwater, WA 98512

**Making Memories**
www.makingmemories.com

**Ma Vinci's Reliquary**
http://crafts.dm.net/mall/reliquary

**Oxford Impressions**
www.oxfordimpressions.com

**Paper Bag Studios**
www.paperbagstudios.com

**Paper Candy**
www.papercandy.com

**Paper Inspirations**
www.paperinspirations.com

**Posh Impressions**
www.poshimpressions.com

**Postmodern Designs, Inc.**
postmoderndesign@aol.com

**River City Rubber Works**
www.rivercityrubberworks.com

**Rubber Baby Buggy Bumpers**
www.rubberbaby.com

**Rubbermoon Stamp Company**
www.rubbermoon.com

**Rubbernecker Stamp Company**
www.rubbernecker.com

**Rubberstamp Ave.**
www.rubberstampave.com

**Serendipity Stamps**
www.serendipitystamps.com

**A Stamp in the Hand**
www.astampinthehand.com

**Stampers Anonymous—The Creative Block**
www.stampersanonymous.com

**Stampington & Company**
www.stampington.com

**Stampland**
www.stamplandchicago.com

**Stampotique Originals**
www.stampotique.com

**Wordsworth**
www.wordsworthstamps.com

**Zettiology**
www.teeshamoore.com

# ...AND MORE

**7gypsies**: a wonderful eclectic collection of papers and embellishments, including the colorwash, attesting the old adage, more is better!
www.7gypsies.com

**All My Memories**: paper embellishments and more!
www.allmymemories.com

**American Tag**: every kind of tag you could want for your paper crafting, plus!
www.americantag.net

**Autumn Leaves**: a vast selection of artistic papers, stickers, and so much more for all your cards, game boards, and scrapbooks.
www.autumnleaves.com

**Bazzill**: Beautiful textured and smooth-finish papers in scrumptious colors for your paper crafts. Embellishments and great idea books, too!
www.bazzillbasics.com

**Blumenthal Lansing Company**:
La Mode buttons and shank removers. Available at local art and craft stores.
www.buttonsplus.com

**Canson**: large sheets of cardstock used for inside the game boards. Available at local art and craft stores.
www.canson-us.com

**Chatterbox**: beautifully coordinated papers, accessories, fonts, and embellishments.
www.chatterboxinc.com

**Colorbök**: assorted papers and embellishments, including metal letters, in various styles for paper art and scrapbooking fun.
www.colorbok.com

**Colorbox**: inkpads—including chalk inks, re-inkers, stamping accessories, and stamp sheets.
www.clearsnap.com

**Creating Keepsakes**: computer software, scrapbooking publications, and much more.
www.creatingkeepsakes.com

**Creative Imaginations**: great source for scrapbook supplies in a variety of styles and themes.
www.cigift.com

**Creek Bank Creations—Twill e dee**: twill tape in various sizes and colors.
www.creekbankcreations.com

**Cropper Hopper**: useful paper- and project-storage products.
www.cropperhopper.com

**Darice**: great supplier for crafting supplies, charms, and more.
www.darice.com

**Deluxe Cuts**: beautiful laser cuts and templates for your scrapbooks, cards, and game boards.
www.deluxcuts.com

**DMC**: beautiful stitching and needlework threads.
www.dmc-usa.com

**DMD Industries—Paper Reflections**: papers, cards, and collage packs in various styles and colors.
www.dmdind.com

**The Envelopes Please** from **Stamp Your Art Out**: envelope templates.
www.theenvelopesplease.com

**Fiskars**: great line of fabric and paper scissors and cutters.
www.fiskars.com

**FoofaLa**: a great, eclectic mixture of tags and embellishments for your artistic creations.
www.foofala.com

**Glue Dots**: a good way to hold embellishments on your cards and game boards.
www.gluedots.com

**Golden Artist Colors**: paints, glazes, and supplies for the serious artist in all of us.
www.goldenpaints.com

**Heidi Grace Designs**: papers and both acrylic and metal embellishments in a variety of sizes and styles.
www.heidigrace.com

**Jacquard**: Lumiere and Neopaque paints.
www.jacquardproducts.com

**JHB Buttons**: novelty, pearl, and metal.
www.buttons.com

**Jolee's By You—EK Success**: wonderful, ready-made embellishments and tools to help you create beautiful artwork. Available at local arts and crafts stores.
www.eksuccess.com

**JudiKins**: along with rubber stamps, they offer diamond glaze, a wonderful dimensional glue, as well as ready-made paper cards and envelopes for you to decorate.
www.judikins.com

**Junkitz**: charms, embellishments, and jump rings for your scrapbooks, cards, and crafts.
www.junkitz.com

**Just Another Button Company**: whimsical and fun buttons for your crafting needs.
www.justanotherbuttoncompany.com

**K&Company**: Life's Journey—beautiful papers, matching accessories, and albums to delight and awe even the most novice paper crafter.
www.kandcompany.com

**Kelly Paper**: source for lining paper in fabric cards.
www.kellypaper.com

**KI Memories**: paper and other scrapbook supplies.
www.kimemories.com

**Lasting Impressions**: sanding blocks, great brads—not to mention all their brass stencils and coordinating papers.
www.lastingimpressions.com

**Li'l Davis Designs**: fun papers and embellishments.
www.lildavisdesigns.com

**Magenta Style**: Maruyama mesh and a wonderful selection of rubber stamps.
www.magentarubberstamps.com

**Magic Scraps**: textured papers, file frames, and other fun embellishments in a variety of styles.
www.magicscraps.com

**Making Memories**: great papers, frames, stamps, ribbons, accessories, and embellishments for your greetings.
www.makingmemories.com

**Marcel Schurman**: embellishments for your creations.
www.schurman.com

**Marcella by Kay**: decorative papers and embellishments; available at Target stores.

**Marvey**: ink pads and punches.
www.uchida.com

**Me & My Big Ideas**: fabric labels, sticker, papers, and more.
www.meandmybigideas.com

**Meri Meri Accents**: fun and hip die cuts for cards and scrapbooks.
www.merimeri.com

**NRN Designs**: a wide range of paper products to meet the needs of life's celebrations.
www.nrndesigns.com

**Offray**: ribbons and trim to adorn your art.
www.offray.com

**Paper Parachute**: beautiful stamps, paper, and metal embellishments for your paper-crafting needs.
www.paperparachute.com

**Provo Craft**: paper, diecutters, charms, embellishments, and stickers.
www.provocraft.com

**Ranger Crafts**: a large selection of craft tools, inks, re-inkers, paints, embossing powders, and much more for all your paper and fabric art creations.
www.rangerink.com

**Tombow**: tape runners.
www.tombowusa.com

**Tsukeniko**: ink pads and re-inkers.
www.tsukeniko.com

**Westrim—Paper Bliss**: wonderful ready-made embellishments and supplies for your card and game board projects.
www.westrimcrafts.com

**Wordsworth**: great selection of wonderful envelope templates complements this company's great offering of stamps, stickers, and paper.
www.wordsworthstamps.com

**Xyron**: sticker, laminate, and magnet machine to aid crafters in all sorts of projects.
www.xyron.com

# GREAT ONLINE FABRIC SHOPS

**The Best Kept Secret**
www.thebestkeptsecret.com

**Big Horn Quilt Shop**
www.bighornquilts.com

**Born to Quilt**
www.borntoquilt.com

**The Cotton Patch**
www.quiltusa.com

**eQuilter.com**
www.equilter.com

**Hancock's of Paducah**
www.hancocks-paducah.com

**Keepsake Quilting**
www.keepsakequilting.com

# GREAT PLACES TO FIND CRAFTING TREASURES

**JoAnn Fabric and Crafts**
www.joanns.com

**Michael's Arts and Crafts Store**
www.michaels.com

**The Stamper's Warehouse**
www.stamperswarehouse.com

# BIBLIOGRAPHY AND SUGGESTED BOOKS

Caldwell, Mary, *Country Living: Handmade Scrapbooks*, Hearst Books: New York City, 1999

Jacobs, Michael and Judy, *Creative Correspondence*, North Light Books: Cincinnati, OH, 2003

Johnson, Robin, *Designing with Vellum*, Leisure Arts: Cincinnatti, OH, 2005

Laury, Jean Ray, *The Fabric Stamping Handbook*, C&T Publishing: Lafayette, CA, 2002

Maryon, Dan, *Designing with Notions*, Sopisticated Scrapbook: Encino, CA, 2005

Miller, Joni K., *The Rubber Stamp Album*, Workman's Publishing: New York City, 1978

Trimble, Erin, *Beyond Attachments*, Making Memories: Centerville, UT, 2004

Trimble, Erin, *Beyond Metal*, Making Memories: Centerville, UT, 2003

Trimble, Erin, *The Book Book* (Designing With…series), Autumn Leaves: Encino, CA, 2004

Trimble, Erin, *Designing with Textures*, Sopisticated Scrapbook: Encino, CA, 2005

# about the author

*Photo by Gregory Case*

Sue Astroth was born in Southern California, where she lived until moving to Concord, CA, in 1997. Sue has been a crafter her whole life—needle arts, quilting, and paper arts are her ongoing favorites. Most recently, she has been combining fabric and paper in unexpected ways.

In 2005 she was fortunate to appear on the 2005 *CHA Craft Special* with Carol Duvall and *Simply Quilts* with Alex Anderson, where she demonstrated her first book, *Fast, Fun & Easy Scrapbook Quilts.*

When she isn't in the studio creating new projects, she is either out collecting treasures for her cards and quilts, pruning her roses in the garden, or working at a local stamp, art, and scrapbook store where she gets lots of great ideas.

Sue doesn't look back . . . except to say thank you to her family and friends for the love and support she constantly receives along her artistic journey.

For more information, ask for a free catalog:
C&T Publishing, Inc.
P.O. Box 1456
Lafayette, CA 94549
(800) 284-1114
Email: ctinfo@ctpub.com
Website: www.ctpub.com

For quilting supplies:
Cotton Patch Mail Order
3405 Hall Lane, Dept.CTB
Lafayette, CA 94549
(800) 835-4418
(925) 283-7883
Email: quiltusa@yahoo.com
Website: www.quiltusa.com

Note: Fabrics and other materials used in the projects shown may not be currently available.